This book belongs to:

Rebecca Penney

It was given to me by:

Mrs. Bouma

On:

Christmas 2011

May the true meaning
of Christmas
always remain
in your heart!

ISBN 978-1-60260-652-4

cover and interior illustration: David Miles

Published by Barbour Publishing, Inc., P. O. Box 719, Uhrichsville, Ohio, 44683 www.barbourbooks.com

Our mission is to publish and distribute inspirational products offering exceptional value and biblical encouragement to the masses.

ecpa Member of the Evangelical Christian Publishers Association

Printed in China

Leo Paper, China; May 2010; D10002349

Christmas Stories for Bedtime

RENAE BRUMBAUGH
ILLUSTRATED BY DAVID MILES

Contents

Frightened!

And the angel said unto her, Fear not, Mary: for thou hast found favour with God. And, behold, thou shalt conceive in thy womb, and bring forth a son, and shalt call his name Jesus.

LUKE 1:30–31

One night, a young girl named Mary was sleeping. Suddenly, a loud voice woke her up! She opened her eyes to a bright light, and she didn't know what was happening. Mary covered her face, wanting to hide from whatever was in her room.

But peeking through her fingers, she saw a beautiful creature all in white.

"Greetings, Mary!" said the angel, whose name was Gabriel. "Don't be afraid. God thinks you are really special. He wants you to be the mother of His Son. You will name Him, 'Jesus.'"

Mary was afraid, and didn't know what to think. She had never seen an angel before. Maybe she wanted to cry, or tell the angel to go away. Maybe she wanted to run away herself! But she didn't. She loved God, and she was willing to do whatever God wanted her to do.

God had a plan to bless Mary, and He wanted to bless the whole world through her. Even though she was frightened, she chose to obey God.

Dear Father, I thank You for sending Jesus. I'm glad Mary obeyed You, even though she was afraid. When I feel afraid, help me to remember that You love me and that I am special to You.

The Angel Gabriel from Heaven Came

The angel Gabriel
from Heaven came,
His wings as drifted snow,
his eyes as flame;
“All hail,” said he,
“thou lowly maiden Mary,
Most highly favored lady,”
Gloria!

“For know a blessèd
mother thou shalt be,
All generations laud and honor thee,
Thy Son shall be Emmanuel,
by seers foretold,
Most highly favored lady,”
Gloria!

Basque carol translated
by Sabine Baring-Gould

The King

He shall be great, and shall be called the Son of the Highest: and the Lord God shall give unto him the throne of his father David: And he shall reign over the house of Jacob for ever; and of his kingdom there shall be no end.

LUKE 1:32–33

Most kings inherit their crowns from their fathers. When a king is born, he is called a prince. Then, when he is old enough, he becomes the king, and he rules over his kingdom. When he dies, or perhaps when he is too old to be a good ruler, one of his sons will become the king.

Sometimes, a king will lose his kingdom altogether. Perhaps there is a war, and another country steals his kingdom away. Or perhaps the people of his own kingdom decide they want a different king.

Jesus is a different kind of king, for His kingdom will never end. He is called the Prince of Peace, but He is also the King of Kings. He has always been the king, and He always will be.

He is a good and kind ruler. He will never die, so He will never have to pass His crown on to anyone else. And no matter who may try to take His kingdom from Him, they will never win. The kingdom of God will remain forever, and Jesus will always be its ruler.

Dear Father, thank You for sending Jesus to be a good and kind ruler. I'm glad He is the king, and that His kingdom will last forever.

There's a Song in the Air

There's a song in the air!
There's a star in the sky!
There's a mother's deep prayer
And a baby's low cry!
And the star rains its fire
While the beautiful sing,
For the manger of Bethlehem
Cradles a King!

There's a tumult of joy
O'er the wonderful birth,
For the virgin's sweet boy
Is the Lord of the earth.
Ay! the star rains its fire
While the beautiful sing,
For the manger of Bethlehem
Cradles a King!

BY JOSIAH HOLLAND

Adopted

Now the birth of Jesus Christ was on this wise: When as his mother Mary was espoused to Joseph, before they came together, she was found with child of the Holy Ghost.

MATTHEW 1:18

Mary and Joseph were planning to get married. They were excited about the wedding. They probably had a big celebration planned, with many guests and a delicious feast. Like most couples, they looked forward to having children some day.

But then Mary and Joseph learned that their first child would be God's Son! They would be parents sooner than they expected.

Jesus had two fathers. Joseph was His adopted father. Joseph loved Jesus, and he taught Jesus all the things that a good father teaches his son.

Joseph taught Him how to be a carpenter and how to be a good man. But God was Jesus' father, too. It was important for everyone to know that Jesus was truly God's Son. God sent Him as a gift to the world.

Just as Joseph adopted Jesus and raised Him as his own son, God wants to adopt each of us to be His children. He loves us, and He will teach us the things we need to know in life.

Dear Father, thank You for sending Your very own Son as a gift to the world. Just as Joseph adopted Jesus, I know You want to adopt me and make me Your own child. Thank You for loving me and teaching me how to live.

Ye Sons of Men, Oh, Hearken

Ye sons of men, oh, hearken:
Your heart and mind prepare;
To hail th'almighty Savior,
Oh sinners, be your care.
He who of grace alone
Our Life and Light was given,
The promised Lord from Heaven,
Unto our world is shown.

Prepare my heart, Lord Jesus,
Turn not from me aside,
And grant that I receive Thee
This blessèd Adventide.
From stall and manger low
Come Thou to dwell within me;
Loud praises will I sing Thee
And forth Thy glory show.

BY VALENTIN THILO,
TRANSLATED BY ARTHUR RUSSELL

New Dad

But while he thought on these things, behold, the angel of the Lord appeared unto him in a dream, saying, Joseph, thou son of David, fear not to take unto thee Mary thy wife: for that which is conceived in her is of the Holy Ghost. And she shall bring forth a son, and thou shalt call his name Jesus: for he shall save his people from their sins.

MATTHEW 1:20–21

Joseph was surprised to learn that Mary was going to have a baby. At first, he wasn't sure if he wanted to adopt her son or not. One night, while he was trying to figure out what to do, he had a dream.

In this dream, an angel spoke to him. The angel said, "Joseph, don't be afraid to make Mary your wife and adopt her son. He is God's

Son, but He will need a dad here on earth. His name will be Jesus, and He will be a blessing to the whole world."

Joseph obeyed God and adopted Jesus. He became Jesus' dad, and he was proud of his son. Sometimes, when we're not sure what to do, we can just wait. If we ask God to help us, He will show us what He wants us to do.

Dear Father, sometimes I don't know what to do. Help me to always look to You for answers. I know that You will help me to do the right thing. Thank You for leading me in the way I should go.

Joseph Dearest, Joseph Mine or Song of the Crib

"Joseph, Dearest Joseph mine,
Help me cradle the Child divine.
God reward thee and all that's thine,
In paradise," so prays the mother Mary.

He came among us at Christmas time
At Christmas time in Bethlehem
Men shall bring him from far and wide,
Love's diadem
Jesus, Jesus;
Lo, he comes and loves and
saves and frees us.

“Gladly dear one, Lady mine
Help I cradle this Child of thine.”
“God’s own light on us both
shall shine,
In paradise,” as prays the
mother Mary.

Traditional German Carol,
14th Century

Choosing a Name

For unto us a child is born, unto us a son is given: and the government shall be upon his shoulder: and his name shall be called Wonderful, Counsellor, The mighty God, The everlasting Father, The Prince of Peace.

ISAIAH 9:6

Before a baby is born, that baby's parents spend a lot of time choosing a name for their child. A name is important, for it will stay with that child throughout life. Often, the parents will choose a name that reflects a positive character trait. Or perhaps they will name their child after someone they admire.

When Jesus was born, He was given many names. Each name tells us something about who He is. He is called Wonderful because He is wonderful. He is called Counselor because He helps us to make good choices.

Jesus is the Mighty God. He is not beneath God—He is God! He is the Everlasting Father. Even those who don't have a father here on earth can claim Jesus as their Father. He will never stop being Father to all who ask.

He is the Prince of Peace. Even when things are scary and unsettled, we can know peace if we know Jesus.

Jesus has many more names, as well. Each name tells us how great He is. Each one lets us know how much He loves us.

Dear Father, thank You for giving Jesus many names, so we could know more about Him. Help me to know and remember all the wonderful things about Him.

Hark! The Herald Angels Sing

Hail, the Heav'n-born
Prince of Peace!
Hail the Sun of righteousness!
Light and life to all He brings,
Ris'n with healing in His wings;
Mild He lays His glory by,
Born that man no more may die;
Born to raise the sons of earth;
Born to give them second birth.

Come, Desire of nations, come!
Fix in us Thy humble home;
Rise, the woman's conqu'ring seed,
Bruise in us the serpent's head;
Adam's likeness now efface,
Stamp Thine image in its place;
Second Adam from above,
Reinstate us in Thy love.

BY CHARLES WESLEY

God with Us

Now all this was done, that it might be fulfilled which was spoken of the Lord by the prophet, saying, Behold, a virgin shall be with child, and shall bring forth a son, and they shall call his name Emmanuel, which being interpreted is, God with us.

MATTHEW 1:22–23

God had promised His people that His Son was coming to be their king. For a long, long time, they had looked forward to Jesus' arrival. They had waited and hoped and prayed. It had been so long, some of them wondered if it was ever going to happen!

But God gave them signs to look for, so they would know Jesus was really God's Son. They were to look for a young girl who was going to have a baby. She would name her son, "Immanuel," which means, "God with us." When those things happened, they would know that God had kept His promise.

When Jesus was born, God truly did come to live with us. Instead of being in heaven where no one could see Him, He became a man. People could now talk to God and touch God and hug God and laugh with God. Because Jesus is God, the people were able to be with Him. When Jesus came, God was really with us!

Jesus was with the people when He was born. Today, God is still with us, watching over us and caring for us. He is all around us, and we can talk to Him any time. He promises to never, ever leave us.

Dear Father, thank You for choosing to be with us. I know I can talk to You any time, and You will never leave me.

Hark! The Herald Angels Sing

Christ, by highest heaven adored,
Christ, the everlasting Lord:
Late in time, behold Him come,
Offspring of a virgin's womb.

Veiled in flesh the Godhead see,
Hail the incarnate Deity!
Pleased as man with men to dwell,
Jesus our Emmanuel.

BY CHARLES WESLEY

Anything Is Possible

For with God nothing shall be impossible.

LUKE 1:37

Mary didn't understand how she could be the mother of God's Son. It didn't seem possible to her. It just didn't make any sense, and she felt confused.

"Don't be confused," the angel said to her. "God can do anything." Then, he told Mary that her cousin, Elizabeth, was going to have a baby, too. Elizabeth was very old, and had never had any children before. It seemed impossible for Elizabeth to have a baby at her age. But God made it happen.

Mary accepted the angel's explanation. She still didn't understand, but she knew that God could do anything. She chose to trust Him, even though it didn't make sense to her. "Okay," she said. "I'll do whatever God wants me to do."

Sometimes, things don't make sense to us. We don't always understand what God is doing. But even when we feel confused, we can trust God. He loves us, and He has great plans for us. He can do anything—nothing is impossible with God. No matter what, we can choose to be like Mary. We can say, "Even though I don't understand, I'll do whatever God wants me to do. I will trust God."

Dear Father, I'm glad to know that nothing is impossible for You. When I feel confused, help me to remember that I can still trust You. When things don't make sense to me, I can trust that You know what You are doing, and You will take care of me.

I Wonder as I Wander

If Jesus had wanted for any wee thing,
A star in the sky or a
bird on the wing,
Or all of God's Angels in
heaven to sing,
He surely could have it, 'cause
he was the King.

I wonder as I wander out
under the sky,
How Jesus the Saviour did
come for to die.
For poor orn'ry people like
you and like I;
I wonder as I wander out
under the sky.

Traditional Appalachian Carol

Regular Person

And Mary said, My soul doth magnify the Lord, and my spirit hath rejoiced in God my Saviour. For he hath regarded the low estate of his handmaiden.

LUKE 1:46–48

When Mary realized that she had been chosen to be the mother of God's Son, she was amazed! She couldn't believe that the God of the universe had chosen her, a young girl, to do such a big job.

She probably thought, *Why did He choose me? I've never done anything important. I'm still young. There are plenty of older, smarter, richer, more important girls. . . . I'm just a regular person. Why didn't He choose someone else?*

But God doesn't look for the important people to do His work. He wants regular people, just like you and me. He wants men and women and boys and girls who live normal lives and work hard and try their best at school. He wants people who love Him and who want to do what He says.

God chose Mary, a young girl, to be the mother of His Son. He chooses you and me to do His important work, as well. Like Mary, we can be excited and amazed, knowing that God notices us, He sees us as important, and He believes we can do His work.

Dear Father, thank You for
giving me important work to do.
I feel honored that You have
chosen me to do special things
for You. I will do whatever
You ask me to. I love You.

The Angel Gabriel from Heaven Came

Then gentle Mary meekly
bowed her head,
"To me be as it pleaseth God,"
she said,
"My soul shall laud and magnify
His holy Name."
Most highly favored lady,
Gloria!

Of her, Emmanuel, the Christ,
was born
In Bethlehem, all on a
Christmas morn,
And Christian folk throughout
the world will ever say—
"Most highly favored lady,"
Gloria!

Basque carol translated
by Sabine Baring-Gould

Good Citizens

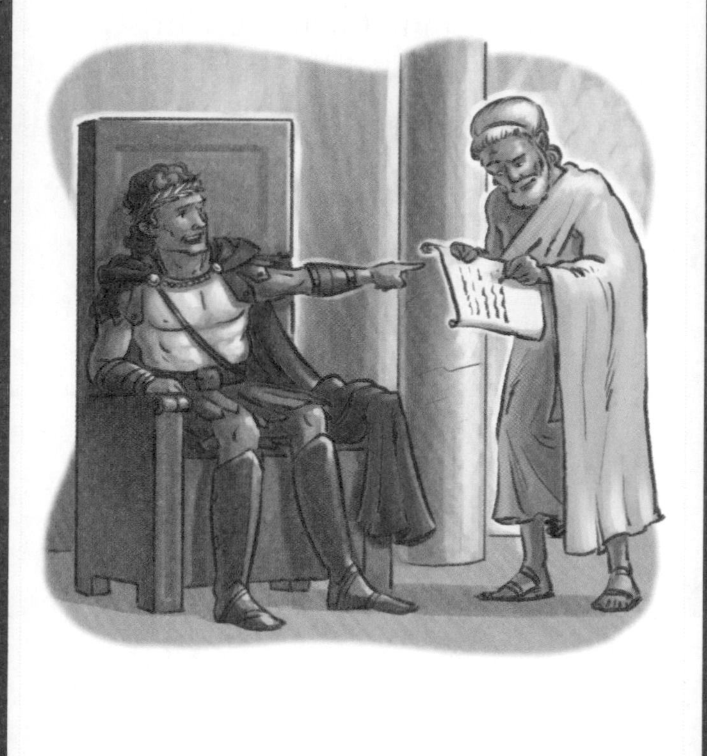

And it came to pass in those days, that there went out a decree from Caesar Augustus that all the world should be taxed. . . . And all went to be taxed, every one into his own city.

LUKE 2:1, 3

Caesar Augustus was the emperor of the Roman Empire. He wanted to know how many people lived in his kingdom. Every few years, he made all the people go to their hometowns so they could be counted.

At that time, travelers packed up enough belongings for a long trip. The people who still lived in their hometowns didn't have far to go. But if anyone had moved away, he or she had to pack food and water and clothes to last for many days. They didn't have cars or trains or airplanes back then. Most of the people had to walk to their hometowns. A few people rode donkeys.

When they got to their hometowns, they registered and told how many people were in their families. This way, Caesar would know how many people lived in his kingdom. He used this information for all sorts of things. It helped him know how many taxes to collect, how many guards to hire, how many roads to build, and other things.

It is important for us to do what our government asks us to do, as long as they don't ask us to disobey God. Governments help countries and kingdoms run more smoothly. God wants us to obey the laws and be good citizens.

Dear Father, thank You for placing people in charge of my government who want to help take care of me. Please give them wisdom as they work to try and make my home a good and safe place to live.

Augustus Caesar Having Brought

Augustus Caesar having brought
The world to quiet peace,
That all the noise of bloody wars
In every land did cease;
Just Joseph, with his Mary mild,
To Bethlehem did come,
Which blessed place appointed was
To ease her burden'd womb.

Then, all the town being
full of guests,
Such was their helpless case,
That not a bed for them was left,

Nor any lodging place;
But in a poor and simple inn,
Even an ox's stall
Appointed was to entertain
The Saviour of us all.

O sing we all, with heart and voice,
Let Christian love increase,
For unto us this day is born
The only Prince of Peace.

BY DAVIES GILBERT

Trust and Obey

And Joseph also went up from Galilee, out of the city of Nazareth, into Judaea, unto the city of David, which is called Bethlehem; (because he was of the house and lineage of David:) to be taxed with Mary his espoused wife, being great with child.

LUKE 2:4–5

Mary and Joseph's families had moved away from their hometown, a place called Bethlehem. Now they lived in the town of Nazareth. Mary and Joseph had to pack up their things and make the long journey back to Bethlehem, so they could be counted. They wanted to be good citizens, so they obeyed their emperor.

It was close to time for Mary to give birth to Jesus, but that didn't matter. She still had to go to Bethlehem to be counted. It was probably a difficult journey for her. She may have wondered why God would ask her to do such a hard thing. But she didn't fuss or complain. She did what she was asked to do. She trusted that God had a reason for making her take that long trip.

Dear Father, sometimes I have to do things I don't want to do. At times, I have to work when I'd rather play, or I have to go to sleep when I want to stay awake. Sometimes I have to take long trips, and sitting in the car for hours isn't fun. Help me to have a sweet attitude. Help me to trust You, even when I don't understand.

O Little Town of Bethlehem

O little town of Bethlehem,
How still we see thee lie!
Above thy deep and dreamless sleep
The silent stars go by;
Yet in thy dark streets shineth
The everlasting Light;
The hopes and fears of all the years
Are met in thee tonight.

For Christ is born of Mary;
And gathered all above,
While mortals sleep, the angels keep
Their watch of wond'ring love.
O morning stars, together
Proclaim the holy birth,
And praises sing to God the King,
And peace to men on earth.

by Phillips Brooks

Mary's Donkey

Joseph also went up. . .to be taxed
with Mary his espoused wife,
being great with child.

LUKE 2:4–5

Clop, clop, clop. The donkey's hooves played a rhythm on the rocky road. Perhaps Mary hummed songs to the rhythm. Perhaps she heard a lullaby and dozed during the long journey.

Bethlehem was a long distance from Nazareth. It took four or five days to travel there, and the roads were rocky and hilly. Most people traveled in groups for safety, because there were often robbers along the trail.

Because Mary was expecting Jesus, it would have been difficult for her to make the journey on foot. She probably rode a donkey. Perhaps she gave him a name and fed him treats. She was probably very grateful for the donkey because, without him, she would have had to walk the entire way.

What a special job that donkey had, carrying God's Son and His mother! The donkey gave his best to God, carrying Mary on the long journey so she wouldn't have to walk. That simple donkey played an important role in God's special plan. God had a plan for Mary, for Joseph, and even for the donkey. He has a plan for you, too. He loves you, and wants you to honor Him by doing your best in everything.

Dear Father, thank You for taking care of Mary on the long journey to Bethlehem. Thank You for sending us animals to love and care for. Mary's donkey gave his best for You. I want to always give my best for You, too.

The Friendly Beasts

Jesus our brother, kind and good,
Was humbly born in a stable rude.
And the friendly beasts around
Him stood,
Jesus our brother, kind and good.
"I," said the donkey, shaggy
and brown,

"I carried His mother up
hill and down;
I carried her safely to
Bethlehem town."
"I," said the donkey, shaggy
and brown.

Traditional English Carol

A Promise Is Forever

[God said to David,] And thine house and thy kingdom shall be established for ever before thee: thy throne shall be established for ever.

2 SAMUEL 7:16

When David was a little boy, he was a lot like all little boys. He helped his family take care of their animals. He liked to play with rocks, and he practiced throwing them at targets. He enjoyed music, and he often sang songs to God.

God liked David, and He thought David would make a good king. He promised David that he would be king one day. But it was a long time before that promise came true. While he was waiting, David might have wondered if God was ever going to keep His promise. But God always keeps His promises, and one day, David became the king.

God promised David that his kingdom would last forever. But it was a long, long time before God made that promise come true. Long after David's death, David's great-great-great (many greats) grandson was born. That baby's name was Jesus. He was in David's family, but He was also God's Son. Through Jesus, God kept His promise to David. Jesus was the King, and He is still the King today. His kingdom will last forever.

God has made promises to us, too. He promises to never leave us. He promises to love us and care for us. And He promises that, if we believe in Jesus, we will spend eternity with Him in heaven. At times, we may wonder if God is going to keep His promises to us. But we never have to wonder about that. God kept His promises to David, and He will keep His promises to us.

Dear Father, thank You for all the promises You gave us. Thank You for always keeping Your promises.

Come, Thou Long-Expected Jesus

Come, Thou long expected Jesus,
Born to set Thy people free;
From our fears and sins release us,
Let us find our rest in Thee.
Israel's Strength and Consolation,
Hope of all the earth Thou art;
Dear Desire of every nation,
Joy of every longing heart.

Born Thy people to deliver,
Born a child and yet a King,
Born to reign in us forever,
Now Thy gracious kingdom bring.
By Thine own eternal Spirit
Rule in all our hearts alone;
By Thine all sufficient merit,
Raise us to Thy glorious throne.

BY CHARLES WESLEY

No Room

There was no room for them in the inn.

LUKE 2:7

Bethlehem was very crowded. Everyone in all the surrounding towns had walked or ridden their donkeys to Bethlehem so they could be counted. Only the first people there were able to find hotel rooms. The others had to sleep outside on the ground. Some of them may have slept in tents.

Joseph wanted Mary to have a warm place to stay. He knew the baby would be born soon, and he didn't want the baby to be born in the cold, windy night air. "Please, sir, can you find a place for us?" he asked the busy innkeeper. He knew how crowded it was, but he was hoping that someone would see that Mary was going to have a baby soon and make room for her.

The kind innkeeper looked at Mary. He wanted to help, but all his rooms were taken! He couldn't kick out any of his customers. After all, they were there first. He didn't know what to do.

Then, he had an idea. "Come with me," he said. "You can stay in my stable. At least it's warm there." He led them to where he kept his animals. It smelled of hay, and the animals probably made noises.

"Baaaa!" said the sheep.

"Mooooo!" said the cow.

Joseph led Mary into the warm stable. He made her comfortable in the hay and thanked God for taking care of his family.

Dear Father, thank You
for always taking care of us.
Even when things don't go exactly
as we planned, we know You
are watching over us.

Thou Didst Leave Thy Throne

Thou didst leave Thy throne
and Thy kingly crown,
When Thou camest to Earth for me;
But in Bethlehem's home was
there found no room
For Thy holy nativity.

O come to my heart, Lord Jesus,
There is room in my heart for Thee.

My heart shall rejoice, Lord Jesus,
When Thou comest and
callest for me.

BY EMILY E. S. ELLIOTT

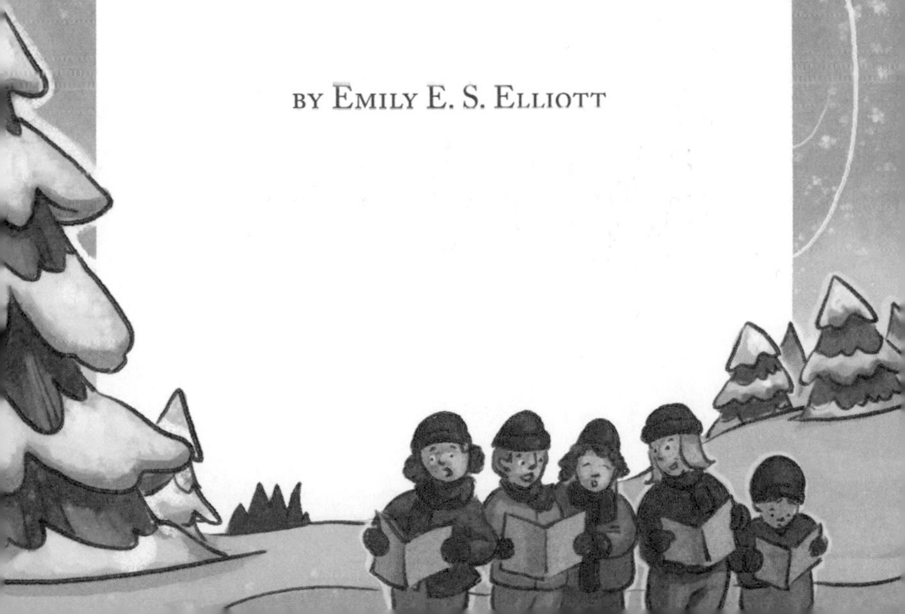

It's Time!

And so it was, that, while they were there, the days were accomplished that she should be delivered.

LUKE 2:6

Joseph and Mary made themselves comfortable in the soft hay of the stable. They may have made friends with the animals there, talking to them and giving them names. Perhaps Mary's own donkey stayed in the stable with them.

Before long, Mary looked at Joseph. "I think it's time," she told him. It was time for Jesus to be born. Since this was their first child, Mary may have felt afraid. Perhaps there was a woman nearby—maybe the innkeeper's wife—who had been through this before. Perhaps she helped Mary to stay calm.

Joseph may have helped, too, or he may have paced back and forth nervously, praying that his wife and the baby would be okay. But he didn't need to worry. The baby who was about to be born was God's Son. God would take care of them.

God's Son, Jesus, was the King of Kings. God could have chosen for His Son to be born anywhere. He could have been born in a huge mansion or a palace. But He wasn't born in any fancy place. He was born in a stable, surrounded by hay and animals. God chose for Jesus to be born in a place where anybody and everybody could find Him.

Dear Father, thank You for sending Your Son as a gift to the world. You didn't hide Him from us, or make it difficult for us to find Him. You promised that everyone who looks for Him will find Him. Thank You for Jesus.

Silent Night! Holy Night!

Silent night, holy night,
Son of God, love's pure light.
Radiant beams from Thy holy face,
With the dawn of redeeming grace,
Jesus, Lord at Thy birth,
Jesus, Lord, at Thy birth.

Silent night, holy night,
Wondrous star, lend thy light;
With the angels let us sing,
Alleluia to our King;
Christ the Savior is born.
Christ the Savior is born.

by Joseph Mohr

Safe and Warm

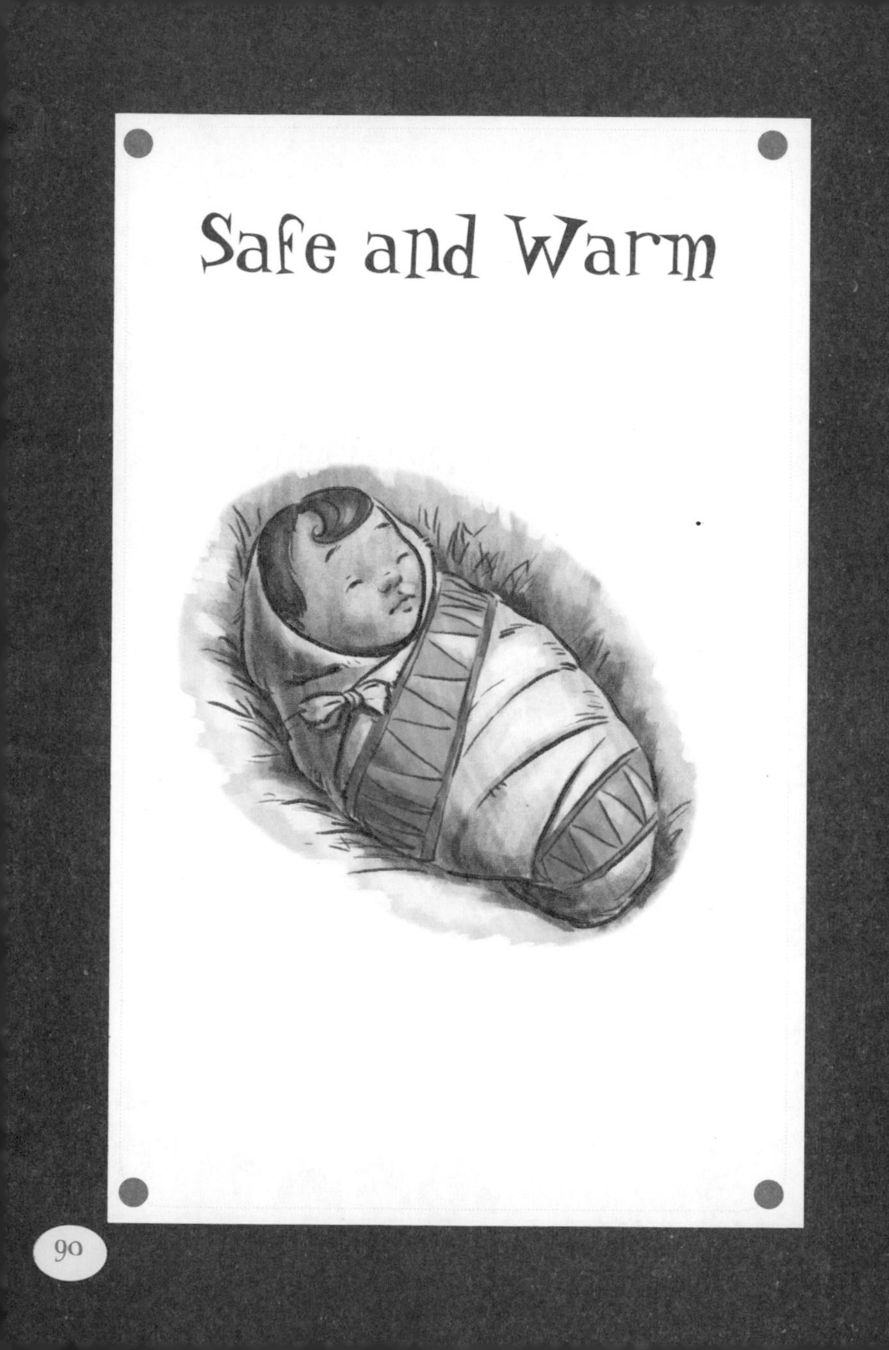

And she brought forth her firstborn son, and wrapped him in swaddling clothes, and laid him in a manger.

LUKE 2:7

Every day, new babies are born all over the world. Every day, the mommies count the tiny fingers and toes of their babies and admire their sweet faces. Then, they wrap the babies tightly in blankets and hold them close. Babies like to be bundled in warm blankets. It makes them feel safe.

Baby Jesus was no different from other babies. His mommy probably counted His fingers and toes. She probably exclaimed over how beautiful and perfect He was. Then, she wrapped Him in soft cloths, or small blankets, and held Him close. Maybe she sang to Him as she fed Him. Perhaps she watched Him fall asleep, then placed Him in a manger.

A manger was a feeding trough for the animals. There was no fancy cradle in the stable, so Joseph may have put fresh hay in the manger. Maybe he laid a clean blanket on top of the hay, to make a soft place for Baby Jesus. Then Mary laid him there. She and Joseph probably sat and looked at Him for a long time, thanking God for giving them a strong, healthy boy.

God provided a warm place for Jesus to be born. He provided a soft place for Jesus to sleep. It may not have been fancy, but it was all He needed. God provides what we need, too.

Dear Father, thank You for always giving me what I need. Help me to be thankful for the good things You give.

While Shepherds Watched Their Flocks

To you, in David's town this day,
Is born of David's line,
The Savior who is Christ, the Lord,
And this shall be the sign,
And this shall be the sign:

The heavenly Babe you
there shall find
To human view displayed,
All meanly wrapped in
swathing bands,
And in a manger laid;
And in a manger laid.

BY NAHUM TATE

The Gift in the Manger

She. . .wrapped him in swaddling clothes, and laid him in a manger; because there was no room for them in the inn.

LUKE 2:7

Chomp, chomp, chomp. The donkeys crunched on the hay filling the manger.

"Baaaa!" A sheep nudged his way in, claiming some of the meal for himself.

Little did the animals know, later that night their feeding trough would hold a great treasure.

When Jesus was born, Mary needed a soft place to lay Him. Because they were in a stable, there were no fancy cradles. She didn't want to lay Him on the ground—He might get stepped on!

"Here, honey. We can lay Jesus in this manger," Joseph may have said. The hay provided a soft cushion, and it kept Him safe from animals' hooves.

Who would have thought that the King of Kings would make His bed in a smelly old feeding trough? This proves that you cannot judge a gift by its package. After all, Jesus was God's most precious gift to the world. And God didn't choose to wrap Him in an expensive, sparkly package. Instead, Jesus was wrapped in simple cloths, and He slept in a manger.

Sometimes, the best gifts are the ones that come in simple packages. They may lack sparkle, but they are filled with love. Those are the gifts that will last and last, even after the package has been discarded.

Dear Father, thank You for the gift of Your love. Thank You, also, for the reminder that Your best gifts often come in simple packages.

Away in a Manger

Away in a manger, no crib for a bed,
The little Lord Jesus laid
down His sweet head.
The stars in the sky looked
down where He lay—
The little Lord Jesus, asleep
on the hay.

The cattle are lowing,
the poor baby wakes,
But little Lord Jesus,
no crying He makes;
I love Thee, Lord Jesus!
Look down from the sky,
And stay by my cradle till
morning is nigh.

SOMETIMES ATTRIBUTED
TO MARTIN LUTHER

Doing Their Jobs

And there were in the same country shepherds abiding in the field, keeping watch over their flock by night.

LUKE 2:8

A shepherd's job is to take care of sheep. It isn't an easy job, for sheep need to be watched all day and all night long, every single day. If a shepherd doesn't do his job, one of the sheep might wander off and get lost or hurt.

There are many dangers to sheep, especially if they become separated from the rest of the flock. They might fall off a cliff and break a bone. Wolves might attack them. Being a shepherd is a demanding job.

On the night Jesus was born, some shepherds were nearby watching over their flocks. Some of the shepherds may have thought, *I'm tired. I don't want to watch over these silly old sheep. Why can't they take care of themselves? I want to go home and go to bed.* But we should always do our jobs, even when we don't feel like it. When we obey God and do what we are supposed to do, He blesses us.

Little did those shepherds know that in a stable nearby, the Son of God was being born. If they had stayed home and not done their jobs that night, they might have missed one of the most exciting nights of their lives!

Dear Father, thank You for blessing me when I obey You. Thank You for giving me important jobs to do. Help me to always do what I'm supposed to do, with a cheerful attitude.

While Shepherds Watched Their Flocks

While shepherds watched their
flocks by night,
All seated on the ground,
The angel of the Lord came down,
And glory shone around,
And glory shone around.

"Fear not!" said he, for mighty dread
Had seized their troubled minds,
"Glad tidings of great joy I bring
To you and all mankind,
To you and all mankind."

BY NAHUM TATE

A Bright Light

And, lo, the angel of the Lord
came upon them, and the glory
of the Lord shone round about them:
and they were sore afraid.

LUKE 2:9

"Baaa, baaa," called the sheep. The shepherds lay on the ground, listening to their flocks and looking up at the stars. Some of them dozed, while others fought to stay awake.

Suddenly, a bright light filled the sky! It lit up the fields and covered the sky as far as they could see.

They placed their arms over their eyes to shield themselves from the bright light. *What in the world is happening,* they must have wondered. It is the middle of the night! *Why is the sky filled with light?*

The light they saw was God's glory. God was happy that His Son had been born, and He wanted the whole world to know. An angel was in the middle of the light. The angel was there as God's messenger, sent to announce Jesus' arrival.

The shepherds were afraid, maybe even terrified! They had never seen anything like this before! Was this a dream? Would the winged creature hurt them? But no, the creature didn't seem angry or mean. It seemed to have something important to tell them. Even the sheep seemed amazed, and they grew quiet.

Although the shepherds were confused, they knew this was a very special night. They looked at the angel, listening for some explanation.

Dear Father, thank You for loving me enough to send Your Son to earth. As I celebrate His birth, help me to be excited about Your love for me.

Angels from the Realms of Glory

Angels from the realms of glory,
Wing your flight o'er all the earth;
Ye, who sang creation's story,
Now proclaim Messiah's birth.

Come and worship,
Comc and worship,
Worship Christ
The newborn King.

BY JAMES MONTGOMERY

A Special Night

And the angel said unto them,
Fear not: for, behold, I bring you good tidings of great joy, which shall be to all people. For unto you is born this day in the city of David a Saviour, which is Christ the Lord.

LUKE 2:10–11

The shepherds had never been so terrified in all their lives. They had been coming to these fields every night for years, and nothing like this had ever happened. Bright lights, winged people in the sky, voices in the air. . .it was unbelievable!

Then the angel spoke to them. “Don’t be afraid! I have good news. What I’m about to tell you will make you very happy.”

The shepherds watched and listened with their mouths hanging open.

The angel continued. “Today in Bethlehem, God’s Son has been born!”

What? How could this be? The shepherds had heard that God was sending a Son. Ever since they were small children, they had been taught about God's promise to their people. But could this really be true? Could God's own Son—the One their parents and grandparents and great-grandparents had waited for—could He really have been born this night, just over those hills?

The shepherds looked at one another. They wanted to know if the others had seen and heard the same thing. Some of them may have pinched themselves to see if they were dreaming. If what the angel said was true, this was truly a special night!

Dear Father, thank You for sending Your angel to tell the shepherds about Jesus. I want to be like that angel, and share Your good news with everyone.

It Came Upon the Midnight Clear

It came upon the midnight clear,
That glorious song of old,
From angels bending near the earth
To touch their harps of gold:

"Peace on the earth,
good-will to men
From heav'n's all-gracious King";
The world in solemn stillness lay
To hear the angels sing.

by Edmund Sears

Searching for the King

And this shall be a sign unto you;
Ye shall find the babe wrapped in
swaddling clothes, lying in a manger.

Luke 2:12

The shepherds were having a hard time believing their own eyes and ears. Bright lights in the sky? Angels? God's Son, born nearby? It was just too amazing to be true.

The angel must have known they needed a sign. "Go see for yourselves!" the angel told them. "Go to Bethlehem and look for Him. You'll find Him wrapped in cloths and lying in an animal's feeding trough."

Again, the shepherds looked at one another. Why, this story was getting crazier and crazier! A feeding trough? A manger? Why on earth would God send His Son, the Prince of Peace, to be born in a stable? Why would God allow the King of Kings to lie in a smelly, dirty manger?

They jumped to their feet and ran to see for themselves, leaving their sheep behind. Over hills they ran, jumping over rocks and small bushes. Good thing God had sent that bright light, so they could see the path!

Into the center of town they ran, darting in and out of stables, not even caring if they woke up the whole city. "Is He here?" they called to one another.

"No, not in this one. Let's try that one over there!"

"Nope. No baby in here."

"Hey, guys! Come over here! I think I've found Him!"

The shepherds followed their friend's voice to the stable. Sure enough, there was a young couple there. And lying in the manger, wrapped in swaddling clothes, was a newborn baby. . .just like the angel said.

Dear Father, thank You for Jesus.

There's a Song in the Air

In the light of that star
Lie the ages impearled;
And that song from afar
Has swept over the world.
Every hearth is aflame,
And the beautiful sing
In the homes of the nations
That Jesus is King!

We rejoice in the light,
And we echo the song
That comes down through the night
From the heavenly throng.
Ay! We should to the lovely
Evangel they bring,
And we greet in His cradle
Our Savior and King!

by Josiah Holland

Feeding the Birds

Consider the ravens: for they neither sow nor reap; which neither have storehouse nor barn; and God feedeth them: how much more are ye better than the fowls?

LUKE 12:24

"Tweet, tweet!" The birds chirp merrily in the trees. They are singing their praises to God. Although they don't have permanent houses, although they don't even have a place to keep their food, God always makes sure they have enough to eat. He takes care of them because He loves them.

On the night Jesus was born, there were animals nearby. They were cared for by their owners, tucked safely into a warm stable. Those owners must have loved their animals. God loves the animals, and He wants us to help Him take care of all of His creatures.

Just as the birds sing praises to God, who takes care of them, the animals in the stable that night may have praised Him for sending the newborn King to be born in their barn.

"Moo," called the cow.

"Baaa," cried the sheep.

"Oink, oink," said the pig.

God loves the animals and cares for them, and He loves us even more. He wants to take care of us. He wants us to trust Him for everything that we need, just as the animals do.

Dear Father, thank You for loving the animals. Please help me to love and care for my animals the way You want me to. Help me to trust You for everything that I need, just as the animals do.

Good Christian Men, Rejoice!

Good Christian men, rejoice
With heart and soul, and voice;
Give ye heed to what we say:
News! News! Jesus Christ is
born today;
Ox and ass before Him bow;
And He is in the manger now.
Christ is born today!
Christ is born today!

Good Christian men, rejoice,
With heart and soul and voice;
Now ye hear of endless bliss:
Joy! Joy! Jesus Christ was
born for this!
He has opened the heavenly door,
And man is blest forevermore.
Christ was born for this!
Christ was born for this!

BY HEINRICH SUSO,
TRANSLATED BY JOHN MASON NEALE

Angels Everywhere!

And suddenly there was with the angel a multitude of the heavenly host praising God, and saying, Glory to God in the highest, and on earth peace, good will toward men.

LUKE 2:13–14

The angel sent the shepherds to Bethlehem. He even gave them a sign to look for, so they'd know they had found God's Son. But before the shepherds could even stand up, the sky filled with angels—more angels than they could count!

These angels weren't talking, though. They were singing! It was the most beautiful music the world had ever heard. Their music filled the skies with praises to God for sending His Son to earth.

"Glory to God!" they sang. "Glory to God in the highest, and on earth peace!"

They knew that Jesus would provide the way for people to have peace with God. Jesus would make it possible for people to have their sins forgiven.

"Peace to men on whom His favor rests," the angels continued. They knew that the only reason God would send His Son to earth was because He loved people so much. God knew that the only way people could have peace was through Jesus Christ.

They sang and sang. We should sing, too, and praise Him every day for loving us.

Dear Father, thank You for loving us so much that You sent Jesus. Thank You for giving me peace. Help me to remember to sing songs to You, out loud and in my heart.

Hark! The Herald Angels Sing

Hark! the herald angels sing,
"Glory to the newborn King;
Peace on earth, and mercy mild;
God and sinners reconciled."

Joyful, all ye nations rise,
Join the triumph of the skies;
With angelic hosts proclaim,
"Christ is born in Bethlehem."

BY CHARLES WESLEY

Spreading the Word

And when they had seen it, they made known abroad the saying which was told them concerning this child.

LUKE 2:17

The shepherds couldn't believe their eyes. They had searched and searched, and they'd found God's Son lying in a manger, just as the angel had said they would. This was the One they had heard stories about. This was the One they had waited their whole lives for. This was the One their parents and grandparents and great-grandparents had waited for.

After spending a few minutes looking at the baby, they knew they couldn't keep this news to themselves. "Let's go tell everyone," they whispered.

With a respectful bow, they slipped out of

the stable. "Thank you for letting us see your baby," they whispered to Mary and Joseph as they left.

As soon as they were outside, they began to walk quickly. Then they began to run. "God's Son is here!" they shouted. "The One we've waited for has been born tonight, right here in Bethlehem! God has kept His promise. The Messiah has come at last!"

People may have stirred from their sleep. "Who is that, waking us up in the middle of the night?" they may have asked.

Some of them arose and went to see for themselves. Others may have pulled the covers over their heads and gone back to sleep. But no matter their response, the shepherds continued to tell everyone they met the good news: Jesus had arrived!

Dear Father, I want to be like the shepherds, telling everyone I know about Jesus.

Bring a Torch, Jeanette Isabella

Bring a torch, Jeanette, Isabella,
Bring a torch, come swiftly and run!
Christ is born, tell the folk of the
village Jesus is sleeping in His cradle.
Ah, ah, beautiful is the Mother!
Ah, ah, beautiful is her Son!

Hasten now, good folk of the village,
Hasten now, the Christ Child to see!
You will find Him asleep
in the manger.
Quietly come and whisper softly.
Hush, hush, peacefully
now He slumbers,
Hush, hush, peacefully now He sleeps.

Traditional French Carol

Mary's Heart

And all they that heard it wondered at those things which were told them by the shepherds. But Mary kept all these things, and pondered them in her heart.

LUKE 2:18–19

"Shhhhh. . ." Mary whispered. "Don't wake the baby." All evening, she had watched a steady stream of visitors file in and out of the stable. It had started with the shepherds. Then, they had told everyone they saw about her new baby. It didn't matter that it was the middle of the night. People were showing up in their night clothes just to get a look at Jesus.

Mary knew that Jesus was special. The angel had told her that He was God's Son. But she still didn't know all that would happen in Jesus' life. She wanted to remember every detail of this night. . .the night she gave birth to the promised Savior.

In many ways, Mary wasn't any different from other mothers. Every mother knows that her baby is special and wants to remember every detail about the day her baby was born. Throughout her baby's life, the mother thinks back on that special time when her child was small.

Later, Jesus went through some very hard things. People were mean to Him. They even killed Him. When those things happened, Mary was very sad. Remembering the sweet things about Jesus' birth and His childhood helped her to feel better. Even though life was hard, she was always glad that God had chosen her to be Jesus' mother.

Dear Father, please help me to remember all the good things about my life. Help me to think about those things when I am sad.

See, Amid the Winter's Snow

Sacred Infant, all divine,
What a tender love was Thine,
Thus to come from highest bliss
Down to such a world as this.

Teach, O teach us, Holy Child,
By Thy face so meek and mild,
Teach us to resemble Thee,
In Thy sweet humility.

BY EDWARD CASWELL AND SIR JOHN GOSS

Anna

[Anna] was a widow of about four-score and four years, which departed not from the temple, but served God with fastings and prayers night and day. And she coming in that instant gave thanks likewise unto the Lord, and spake of him to all them that looked for redemption in Jerusalem.

Luke 2:37–38

Anna was very old. She never had any children of her own, and her husband had died a long time ago. She spent most of her life at the temple, praising God and helping out in any way she could.

She loved God very much, and she wanted to serve Him. She knew one of the best ways to serve God was to stay at the temple. That way, she would be ready if somebody there needed something.

Some people might have grown tired of serving God, but not Anna. She never said, "I think I'll stay home today. I'd rather visit with my neighbors, or sew myself a new dress." She knew she was supposed to be at the temple, serving God. Because she obeyed God, she was at the temple when Mary and Joseph arrived with baby Jesus. She got to hold God's Son, and be among the first to announce His arrival to the world.

Like Anna, we need to serve God and obey Him every day. That way, we will always be where we are supposed to be. We never know when God may choose to show up and bless us.

Dear Father, I want to serve You like Anna did. I love You.

In the Bleak Midwinter

Angels and archangels
May have gathered there,
Cherubim and seraphim
Thronged the air;
But his mother only,
In her maiden bliss,
Worshipped the Beloved
With a kiss.

What can I give him,
Poor as I am?
If I were a shepherd
I would bring a lamb,
If I were a wise man
I would do my part,
Yet what I can I give Him —
Give my heart.

BY CHRISTINA ROSSETTI

The Wise Men

Now when Jesus was born in Bethlehem of Judaea in the days of Herod the king, behold, there came wise men from the east to Jerusalem, saying, Where is he that is born King of the Jews? for we have seen his star in the east, and are come to worship him.

MATTHEW 2:1–2

"Look at that star!" The man pointed, and his friends looked at the sky. The man and his friends were very smart. They had spent years studying the stars. They believed they could learn things about God by watching His creation.

"Do you think that's the one?" asked another man. "Could that be the star that will lead us to God's Son?"

"Let's go find out," replied the first man. The wise men packed up their belongings and left right away. They didn't care how long it took them. They were ready to travel as far as they needed to, so they could see Jesus. After a long time, they found Jesus and his parents. They knew they were in the presence of God's Son.

The wise men looked for Jesus, and they knew they would find Him. We can look for Jesus, too. Oh, we may not see Him in person. Still, we can look for ways that He shows His love to us. We can look for ways to show His love to other people, for when we show His love, Jesus is there.

Father, thank You for sending the wise men to Jesus. I want to be wise, too. I want to spend each day seeking Your love and Your plan for my life.

We Three Kings of Orient Are

We three kings of Orient are,
Bearing gifts we traverse afar
Field and fountain, moor
and mountain,
Following yonder star.

O star of wonder, star of night,
Star with royal beauty bright,
Westward leading, still proceeding,
Guide us to thy perfect light.

BY JOHN H. HOPKINS

King Herod

When Herod the king had heard these things, he was troubled, and all Jerusalem with him.

MATTHEW 2:3

The wise men traveled a long time looking for Jesus. They had to stop to rest and for food and water. When they stopped, they talked to the people who lived in that place. "We're looking for the newborn king," they said excitedly.

One night, they stopped in King Herod's town. When Herod heard the men were looking for the king of the Jews, he was concerned. *I'm the king*, he thought. *Who is this baby they are looking for?* He became worried that someone was trying to take his job from him.

Herod wanted to find out who this baby was. He wanted to make the baby and his family go away, so they wouldn't try to take his job. He didn't understand that Jesus' kingdom wasn't here on earth.

Herod pretended to be interested in baby Jesus. He told the men, "When you find the baby, come back and tell me where He is, so I can send Him a present. I want to worship Him, too."

But Herod didn't really want to send a gift. He didn't really want to worship Jesus. He wanted to kill Him.

If Herod had only taken time to find out more about this baby, he would have known that Jesus didn't come to be an earthly king. He came to be the King of our hearts.

Dear Father, thank You for sending Jesus to be the King of my heart. I want to worship You with my life.

The Birthday of a King

In the little village of Bethlehem,
There lay a Child one day;
And the sky was bright
with a holy light
O'er the place where Jesus lay.

Alleluia! O how the angels sang!
Alleluia! How it rang!
And the sky was bright
with a holy light.
'Twas the birthday of a King.

BY WILLIAM H. NEIDLINGER

Following the Star

When they had heard the king, they departed; and, lo, the star, which they saw in the east, went before them, till it came and stood over where the young child was. When they saw the star, they rejoiced with exceeding great joy.

MATTHEW 2:9–10

"There it is. Let's go that way!" one of the wise men called to his friends. "I think we're getting closer."

The wise men traveled for a long time. Night after night, month after month, for more than two years they followed that star! The star kept moving, guiding them to where they needed to be. At times, they probably grew tired. They may have wondered if they would ever reach their destination. Maybe they even thought about turning around and going home.

But they kept going. They didn't give up. Finally, the star stopped over the house where Jesus lived with His parents. They couldn't believe their eyes! Was their journey finally coming to an end?

As the wise men approached the house, they were filled with joy. At last, they would see the One they had searched for! At last, they would meet God's Son, Jesus. They knew this was a very special day, indeed.

The wise men followed the star. They went where God led them, and He gave them joy. When we follow God, He helps us to feel joyful, too.

Dear Father, I'm glad the wise men followed where You led them. I want to follow You, too.

The First Noel

The first Noel the angel did say
Was to certain poor shepherds
in fields as they lay;
In fields where they lay
keeping their sheep,
On a cold winter's night
that was so deep.

And by the light of that same Star,
Three wise men came from
country far;
To seek for a King was their intent,
And to follow the Star
wherever it went.

Old English carol

Gifts for Baby Jesus

And when they were come into the house, they saw the young child with Mary his mother, and fell down, and worshipped him: and when they had opened their treasures, they presented unto him gifts; gold, and frankincense and myrrh.

MATTHEW 2:11

The wise men could hardly believe their eyes! They had traveled for so long, and at times they had wondered if they would ever reach the new King. But there in front of them was a house. The star they had followed stood still, directly over that house. They knocked on the door, and Mary answered. "May I help you?" she asked.

"We're here to see God's Son. Is He here?"

"Yes, He is." She invited them in. Maybe she offered them something to eat or drink. But no matter how tired and thirsty the men were, they probably had only one thing on their minds. They wanted to see God's Son!

Jesus was about two years old. Perhaps He was eating His lunch, or building with some blocks. The men came right in and knelt down in front of Jesus.

They gave Him gifts, too. The gifts were expensive gifts, suitable for a king. Jesus was too young to understand how nice the gifts were. Mary thanked them and put the gifts away, for when Jesus was older.

We can give Jesus gifts, too. Oh, we may not have fancy gifts like the wise men gave. But the thing Jesus wants most is our hearts. When we love Him with our whole hearts, we give Him the most precious gift of all.

Dear Father, I love You. Please help me to love You more each day, with my whole heart.

The First Noel

This Star drew nigh to the northwest,
O'er Bethlehem it took its rest,
And there it did both stop and stay,
Right over the place where Jesus lay.

Then entered in those
wise men three,
Full rev'rently upon their knee,
And offered there in His presence,
Their gold, and myrrh, and
frankincense.

Old English carol

The Greatest Gift

For God so loved the world, that he gave his only begotten Son, that whosoever believeth in him should not perish, but have everlasting life.

JOHN 3:16

Christmas is a fun time, filled with surprises and brightly wrapped gifts. Everywhere we go, we see beautifully decorated wreaths and hear festive music. Christmas brings fun secrets and delicious food. For many people, Christmas is the most wonderful time of the year.

The colorful trees are pretty, but they aren't the reason we celebrate Christmas. The music is nice to listen to, but it's not the reason for Christmas either. The gifts are fun to open, but even they are not the reason we celebrate Christmas. The purpose of the season is not about the gifts we receive on Christmas morning. It's about the gift that God gave a long time ago.

Jesus is the reason we celebrate Christmas. The word *Christmas* actually comes from His name—Christ. We celebrate Christmas because God loved us so much that He sent His Son, Jesus, to live with us. Jesus lived His life for us, so we could see how to live. Then He gave His life for us, to take the punishment for our sins. No matter how great the new bicycles and the dolls and the games and the new puppies may seem, none of those gifts compares to the true gift of Christmas: Jesus Christ.

God gave us a gift, and we can give a gift back to Him. He loves us, and He wants us to love Him, too. When we choose to love Him with our whole hearts, we give Him the perfect gift.

Dear Father, thank You for giving the greatest gift of all time—Your Son.

O Little Town of Bethlehem

How silently, how silently
The wondrous Gift is giv'n!
So God imparts to human hearts
The blessings of His Heav'n.
No ear may hear His coming;
But in this world of sin,
Where meek souls will receive
Him still,
The dear Christ enters in.

O holy Child of Bethlehem,
Descend to us, we pray;
Cast out our sin and enter in,
Be born in us today.
We hear the Christmas angels
The great glad tidings tell—
O come to us, abide with us,
Our Lord Emmanuel.

BY PHILLIPS BROOKS

Feeding the Sheep

Lovest thou me? . . . Feed my sheep.

John 21:17

At Christmas, we think about Jesus, God's gift to us. We think about giving gifts to others, and we take extra effort to make those gifts special. We save our money, we wrap the gifts in shiny paper, and we wait with excitement for those gifts to be opened.

But Jesus wants us to be gift-givers every single day. He wants us to share the gift of His love with everyone we meet. After all, people need to know that He loves them all the time, not just at Christmastime! They need His love each day of their lives.

In a way, Jesus wants us to be like the shepherds in the Christmas story. The people we meet are like the sheep. He wants us to care for them and feed them with His love. When we do that, we give them the greatest gift. We also give Jesus a gift, too, as we do what He asks us to do.

Dear Father, I love You, and I want to feed Your sheep. Help me to share Your love with everyone I meet, all year long.

O Holy Night

Truly He taught us to
love one another,
His law is love and His
gospel is peace.
Long live His truth,
and may it last forever,
For in His name all discordant
noise shall cease.

Sweet hymns of joy in
grateful chorus raise we,
With all our hearts we
praise His holy name.
Christ is the Lord! Then ever,
ever praise we,
His power and glory ever
more proclaim!
His power and glory ever
more proclaim!

Traditional French Carol

About the Author

Renae Brumbaugh is an author and syndicated columnist with more than two hundred articles in print. She lives in Texas, where she juggles being a pastor's wife, mom to Charis and Foster, and teaching seventh grade Language Arts at the local junior high.